MW00813009

MUSEUM *of* DISTANCE

MUSEUM *of* DISTANCE

POEMS BY ASHLEY SEITZ KRAMER

ZONE 3 PRESS

Clarksville, Tennessee

ZONE 3 PRESS | Clarksville, Tennessee

Copyright © 2015 by Zone 3 Press
All rights reserved

FIRST PRINTING

All rights reserved. No part of this book may
be reproduced in any form or by any electronic or
mechanical means including information storage
and retrieval systems without permission in writing
from the publisher, except by a reviewer.

Library of Congress Cataloging-in-Publication Data

Kramer, Ashley Seitz.
  [Poems. Selections]
  Museum of distance : poems / Ashley Seitz Kramer.
    pages cm
  ISBN 978-0-9906333-1-0 (alk. paper)
  I. Title.
  PS3611.R346A6 2015
  811'.6--dc23
                              2015011281

ISBN: 978-0-9906333-1-0

Book and Cover Design by **David Bieloh**
Cover Art: "Enigma of Dreams" © 2012
by **Honora Jacob**

A Tennessee Board of Regents Institution

Austin Peay State University does not discriminate on the basis of race, color, religion,
creed, national origin, sex, sexual orientation, gender identity/expression, disability, age,
status as a protected veteran, genetic information, or any other legally protected class
with respect to all employment, programs and activities sponsored by APSU.

for Eric

for my parents

| CONTENTS

CONTENTS

CONTENTS

INTRODUCTION

Ashley Seitz Kramer's poems are your new familiars. Call on them to "lively up yourself," as Bob Marley says it. Texting a friend to hear news, we aren't seeking raw fact, but a viewpoint. In need of emotion, we hear a particular take, and the take is the takeaway.

Since these poems make the familiar fresh again, hearing them describe what's here is vital.

On origin:

When I read *origin* I see opening: wounds
oozing deep in the fur, the beginning
of sympathy.
                    (from "Origin & the Apple Bruised")

On joy:

Here's to that moment of joy
when the boat opened the sea
the sea opened the sail
and the sail billowed: a broken neck
in a bright blue kite sky.
                    (from "Between Land & Water")

On fear:

I have no proof of my own fear
without these: the shoulders
of the moose crossing our trail
mid-day: deadly & indifferent
to us & the neon cottonwoods
shocking October.
                    (from "Proof")

On misfortune:

. . . Does anyone
comfort anyone else as we pay on swelling debt? The children
I might have had are somersaulting across the backyards
of the city's ugliest houses and the river has exchanged its faithful tributary
for a new one. My friend the painter reminds me that everything
is a cycle: add a color to another color and another color comes.
I'm trying to savor every hue, like butter melting into yesterday's bread,
but what can I expect from myself or my allies full of grace
for the people who bag their groceries? *Don't crush the eggs.*
Don't crush the raspberries. In light of the many and simple laws
of physics, how can we call each other any closer?
(from "The Wind Carried Him as It Carried Me")

On longevity:

The streetlight will last as long
as the ocean will last as long
as the sun burning what I love.
(from "The Science of Longevity")

In these poems

There is room for every nervous creature, each timid
limb reaching toward the edge of the mossy sheen that
fringes a forgotten pond, the one you can envision but no
longer visit.
(From "Hymn for the Leaping Pig")

Bees produce words, pronounce judgments:

>   … In the mornings
> they chant *viscosity viscosity*. In the evenings
> they distinguish shades of amber. It's heartbreaking.
> The bees hold court in secret behind the barn near
> pea shoots.
>   (from "I Call to the Bees")

Like all good friends, these poems don't withhold what they want:

> I want this line to be long the way sleep is long because the man I love is missing
> from his body. He can't find himself without leaving his body, which he keeps
> forgetting. He drifts toward Lamb's Canyon on his bike and I search the line
> for his headlight, for him, but we're both forced to go back to the beginning.
>   (from "A Cup of Salt Consumes the Sea")

> If only I could build a house
> with what has been left, to use
> what has been judged
>
> unusable, to be then like the island
> making a pyramid
> from a puddle of earth.
>   (from "Breathing Down the House")

In the poems of Ashley Seitz Kramer, as in all fine poetry, message is the
apotheosis of articulation, as what is said and how it is said become one.
Here, the realized "how" delights, and how: a dance so brightly entangled
with its dancer that we want it to see into us, believe it somehow does.

Angela Ball
The University of Southern Mississippi

MUSEUM *of* DISTANCE

THE EVOLUTION OF IDEAS

I invented a beginning, pulled it through the eye
of a needle, pressed it into plumage

which I haven't yet seen fly. I saved it
from the darkness at the end. I see

how a single tree in the field stands
for itself. It brightens and dies, a pinwheel

made from yellow grass. The beginning
is small. I come from that place.

SHORTCOMING

It's not your fault the boy fell
loop by loop through the universe
of unaffordable fears, through the indigo
stripe. He plucked the chewed gum
from the sand and he ate it and oh my god
refused to spit it out. Now loners on the beach
stretch to lotion their own backs and they miss
most of everything big time and tomorrow
it will show because the rhythm of error was written
centuries ago. When the jury reconvenes, each
member looks hungry, somehow sunburned.
What they agree on is this: pink is pervasive, it's ruining us.
Old people scale the earth with metal detectors
and they don't find much. It's a surprise to everyone
that the cucumber plants are strong enough to strangle
but people will always make jokes about the things
that are the most unfunny. The grass leans
toward a desperate shade of death, the tomatoes hang
too heavy for their own houses and that kite
which is otherwise wide is thinning to its younger self
and heading straight for those trees, but true: that sombrero
asked to be sat on. The picnic improves with your theories,
guests delight in your salsa-flavored superstitions.
High heels are dangerous and that is that.
So are slippers. So are earrings.
Crawling *is* preferable to climbing. That horizon
does take you in and the headlines are bigger
than the breeze which knows a person over and over
and the rain is uncontrollable, so yes, damn the cancer.
You do not clamor nor are you savvy.
My own impossible future is a Ferris wheel.
My brother coughs and what comes up is Leviticus.

My horoscope is accurate and ominous, my hair
is darkening into the night and my hands are always
losing each other and I am always lost and looking
for them and I can't hear my own laughter or yours
or anyone's really. I crave the defenses of the Saguaro
cactus. I'm not saying the facts are wrong,
I'm saying I don't believe them. I'm blinder
than I knew and strange enough.

CORROSION THEORY

Go on, stranger, pass through.
You're welcome here but you aren't
safe. There's a woman whose face
was burned in a kitchen fire, a child with scars
for arms. Empathy runs through our bodies
like motor oil, but have I mentioned
the feverish rust? It spreads from one wheel arch
to another, from one small bolt to a panel
to a hood—broad with begging, smooth
with newness—to an entire life flaking
into the hard grey ground. In Mechanicsburg
the flies are bigger but they move
slowly: nothing is chasing them. No one
looks up here, not to talk to God, not to throw
sneakers over the phone lines, not to predict rain,
not even to worry the birds, neon bright
on their branches which are held out like fishing
poles over a shallow pool of shavings
that glows and glows in the early hours.

PERSISTENCE OF VISION

My empathy is anonymous & carries
no cane. My empathy is red, a color Lillian

can find in a crowd. I see the scaffolding
that rested, so she thought, on that man's

shoulders. The fire engine sliced in two,
the woman on the street with splinters in her eyes—

just oaks across the road.
May the lord relieve your daily terror.

Bring down the pontoon chimera floating
in the river of a traffic jam. The barn is now

a diagram but let the hawk be true.

ASTONISHMENT FOR THE SPARROWS

I divided my smallest error by my greatest deed.
Nearby I kept the most beautiful cages
to recall everything I might contain, not much.
During a solstice, I painted your last reliable map
on the back of my hand, its freckled topography.
I followed small rivers of veins to vast pastures of paleness.
When I converted foot-candles to lux, I noticed how
the light only fell where you laid it down. Secretly
I doubted the idea of measurement—its instruments,
my own. I did not want to forget a single thing
you ever told me even though eventually you wouldn't—
couldn't—still mean each thing. This is how we live forever
in our own minds amid formulas for space and time,
despite the ice and innocent forgeries and with astonishment
for the sparrows who carry their houses in their mouths and
build them quietly again without us: each mouth an engineer,
each airy switch a memory to artfully stitch in, each house
a museum of difficult distances. Sometimes it seems cruel
that the truth erodes itself, sometimes it seems kind.

across the tossed fruit
we first ate from

through our orange bedroom
with the faded blinds
through our blindness—

the Wednesdays and the Saturdays
of our twenties now passing.

Call me down to the floor
like a starfish you loved once
for too many arms.

THE STORM, MY CHEST SO CLOSE TO THE SPADE

I warmed the Nagano bulbs in my palm.
Asked each one to live deep and grow tall.
My hands were in the dirt, my fingers
finding roots, my sweat the rain we'd needed
for weeks. When my knees were tender
from kneeling, my chest so close
to the spade, the lightning seized me: my dark
hair was not streaked white but my voice
fluttered from me, a wounded bluejay—
I planted it in the opened earth. Later I sang
in the shower and woke my wife. My students
marked the chalkboard; their equations made me
shake. *Can you use a toaster?* they asked. *Can you
play tricks with the light switch? You're unpredictable, even sitting
in a chair!* I began to dream about the cooler waters,
my grandma baking lemon squares, my father's red truck
catching fire on a midnight drive. I saw a garden, mine,
and walked its rows of tulips. I saw the sun, orange,
someone's mother's favorite scarf. I saw a scarf
soft to the touch. My wife's pale and starry stomach.
I saw my tulips and their faces opened.
How and when do we divide by one? I cut them
at the stem and I kept them on my desk.

PROOF

I have no proof of my own fear
without these: the shoulders
of the moose crossing our trail
mid-day: deadly & indifferent
to us & the neon cottonwoods
shocking October. You
seem already sad & I can't be
trusted—I double what the recipe
calls for when it comes to onions.
I cry & cry & feel cleaned out.
I have no proof
without him, the man
on the motorcycle who died
within minutes of my father
finding him on a back road
in southern Ohio. After the wreck,
against the fence. He's borrowed
time before he says & now—
Addison, eight pounds, is alive
& thriving, one week new
to this world in which two
young boys, strangers,
offer to help carry my couch & later
in the same day, a man
threatens to poison my dog.

THE SCIENCE OF LONGEVITY

I have not positioned my body just so
in a dark, dry place or waited
three to six weeks.

When I was seven
I was praised but everything
has been an effort.

I don't use numbers because
they make more sense than words—
I don't use words because they help me to speak.

The streetlight will last as long
as the ocean will last as long
as the sun burning what I love.

DIAGRAM INCLUDING TIME & BANANAS

The young couple on the porch
is making a plan in the middle
of an ordinary month
as the Goldenrain grows without
interruption, limb by slender limb.
Part of the plan involves each person,
separately, the way the earth prefers
one seed at a time, each seed weighing
as much as the long blond braid
of the pretty girl who walks past the house
in the evenings, every evening,
walking and walking right into the sun
which rests in each crevice of her collarbone.
When someone waves to her
she waves back. Part of the plan
involves time which suggests itself
as an answer for almost every question
any couple could ask. What else
could govern the rules that govern
even the Goldenrain, its veins nursing
on the lackluster soil of a new century
overwhelmingly complex like all the others?
It is no surprise that part of the plan
involves the house, large for its choices.
Inside: narrow doorways, the water
spots on silverware, the fitted sheet
loosening its grip. The bananas are perfect
only at night and only for one night.

NEIGHBOR

I feel it when I'm pouring milk
or folding towels against my chest or passing

the house where a boy is cutting
grass, long hair hanging down in his face.

Do you think he wants to be unfound
or missing or that he's holding

out for something better?
If he went away

would he come back?
Fruit flies are rising from the sink

in search of rotten bananas.
You're looking away & out & through

the dry air. I need to know that you could
see this boy should he be running

down the street & call to him
should he need directions. I need

to know you could hear him
should he knock & need a new life

or a small loan—which he is good for.

TRAGEDIES NEAR WEEPING ROCK

Ignore the babbling teens & deafening echoes
  of nailpolish comparisons. Let us mourn
the death of the condor's mate. He searches
  for her now in every dappled canyon
but we know the rangers found her body
  days ago. Nature watches us settle
into the desert's deep red. Here we are
  among the piñon pines & dotting
the plains, our only hope a porch
  light in what feels like too far a distance.
We could walk to that one wink of light
  & one day we might along the road
I'm tracing now with my finger—
  it moves across the darkening land
at a farmer's mile per second. Nature
  says *proceed*. Abandon any doubts
as they are useless in these falling temps.
  There was a zebra at the last gas station
& a woman who ate an entire burrito
  as big as three fists without so much as
glancing at her son, not once. The road cuts
  across the covered acres of my coming years
then disappears under what is now a half-eaten
  moon. It's all I can do to keep my eyes on it,
several minutes straight now. Someone tried
  in earnest to describe the mountains to you.
It was me but still a mistake.

I CALL TO THE BEES

I make myself known but I walk
among them with an argument swelling, the fields
full of flowers spreading grain by grain
on their backs. What is as simple? What sustains,
what pours forth. I admire the hive's single
entrance: few words can fit through. In the mornings
they chant *viscosity viscosity*. In the evenings
they distinguish shades of amber. It's heartbreaking.
The bees hold court in secret behind the barn near
pea shoots. The sun is a spotlight. I hear the sound
inside of what's hollow: well-made plans, a choir
of clapping. I move slowly still.

A CUP OF SALT CONSUMES THE SEA

I want this line to be long the way sleep is long because the man I love is missing
from his body. He can't find himself without leaving his body, which he keeps
forgetting. He drifts toward Lamb's Canyon on his bike and I search the line
for his headlight, for him, but we're both forced to go back to the beginning.
I thought I was dreaming when a rack of clothes toppled onto a man
at the department store waiting patiently for his daughter, studier of coats.
She unburied him: a dusty jewel, a pumpkin-colored sweater. And the man at the gym
who fell on his elbow wants the line to be long enough for his aching
because his aching is complex and now his knee feels funny too.
His wife is dead. He was unprepared for all the leftovers. It's obvious
he doesn't trust the line now, what it promises and how it surprises even the most
prepared among us—including our fathers, who need their knees replaced.
Sometimes I need to fill up the whole room with my own voice knowing
there's no room left for my body, or other bodies, or my cat and the knots in her body.
I need to speak and speak and hope I can hear a clue that wasn't there before.
Where am I *really?* What do I want? What can I trust if I can't trust the very line
that requires me? It's easier to wear red, to park at the far end of a dark lot,
to pretend it's a wheat field and the wheat is at my shoulders, to believe
the line could follow me—even this far.

ORIGIN & THE APPLE BRUISED

No, this is not a wound. This is an origin.
                    Muriel Rukeyser

When I read *origin* I see opening: wounds
oozing deep in the fur, the beginning
of sympathy. Who can hear that? I enter
the house: applause from an empty kitchen.
In my one hand, an apple bruised by the week.
The sound my diligent mouth makes eating
an apple. I chew, I swallow, I hear that too.
In my other hand, the wrinkled idea of Eve.
I listen for the air of altitude before I memorize
the quiet—each barrow carries a note. I depend
on my deafness now as I retreat from the golden door
handles. I light candles already lit. I call up the stairs,
sing down the stairs, imitate my own echo. I watch
my mouth, now craving the skin of apples, move
in the foyer mirror, never understand the thing
I call sound: it has come from within *me*,
spilled from *my* throat, been taken back
in through my own openings—I mean,
origins—I mean, wounds.

BREATHING DOWN THE HOUSE

If only I could build myself a house
As far away as possible from
Myself.
                        Marin Sorescu

If only I could build myself
a house with feathers then breathe
it down. I'd build it

on a Tuesday. I'd forget
to make a door. I'd unfold the briefest
memories like stiffened sheets

and then could I ask myself
any kind of question? Would I hear
the echo of an answer? If only I could

build myself a house with peaches
then eat it down or be a house
myself then wear it down with walking

or treading water or breaking bread
against my face. If only I could spin
a house from silk, unbury

the house that lay beneath this
one, soak it up to the surface
with crackers, spit it all back out.

If only I could build a house
with what has been left, to use
what has been judged

unusable, to be then like the island
making a pyramid
from a puddle of earth.

EACH LEG A GOOD ROOT

I was born in a tunnel halfway through
   Lent, so my mother gave me up to the earth
above. My father found me years later growing
   leaves under the shadow of a great big pine
who taught me how to breathe & wasn't
   disappointed that I wasn't blessed with needles.
I slept on a bed of fallen hair until I was brave
   enough to crawl. When I was brave enough
to walk, I gathered up my mother's gifts & spread
   them out in places that grew grey instead of green.
I still dream of being pulled down & kept close.
   Mostly I dream of being olive & emerald, chartreuse,
each leg a good root. My sister is a clown
   with pillows for arms. She holds me sometimes.
She cries in her sleep but I never mention it. I cry too
   so we can feel close. I made my own bicycle
from cereal boxes & I let her ride on the half-eaten
   handlebars, even though she's bigger than me,
even though I squint less than she does when it's sunny
   outside or when it's dark like God threw down
a thick black curtain. *Abracadabra.* I let her be my eyes.
   I made a photograph from broken seashells.
I made a bat-house from orange peels. I started
   my own school, which is well-attended by the doves.
When strangers ask if I'm hungry
   I reach down & pat the grass. Father asks if Mother
will come back for us & I yawn a yeah. Aunty asks
   if I've found what I'm looking for. I look up
at the sky & sneeze every time. She understands.
   She washes the plastic spoons. Once someone asked
me about my favorite color, but I didn't understand
   the question. I offered a handful of seeds instead:
each with a desire to sprout, each with genuine thirst.

HOUND

You circle your own house with your dog
who knows when to sit before you ask him
as if both of you learned the same word
in different languages. You trust his language
more. He wakes when you wake dreaming
about the same high grasses. Another word.
No one knocks now when the snow
makes of you a warmer planet. So much
for the terror of your first child's first seizure.
So much for the collision of cars, the spray
of glass, a brown belt left on the seat of a blue van
at the bodyshop. *Did those people make it?*
No. This kind of terror takes years to be made
like the fog that has settled on all the kitchen
tumblers. First the water, then its reason.
It takes years to arrive and when it does
even your dog, who is otherwise oblivious
to history and always a *good boy*, will whimper
for you in your own terrible language.

I AM STEADILY INCREASING

Once I was a melody whispered
in a teacup, my echo
unfettered but fragile

and now I am more.

I span the codes, my hands
the latitudes. I am taller, somewhat large
in my containment of winter rain.

I gather the sun in my dark mouth.
The month passes like a gasp
in the throat. I orbit no one.

The air around me moves
like the spiral arms of a tropical storm
waving and waving
to the eye of the earth.

Someone is a mother here, surely,
someone is called *mother*,
but not me. That's not how
I'm strong. My legs

are not long but still they stretch
the spectrums of color and sound

I resound all the greys
and the greens, from pale to deep,
and yes, of course the blues:
I am true to you.

I am steady

I am increasing, my shadow
introduces other shadows to the sea
and when they wade out far—

too far to call back in
the edges blur
but I await them all
each shadow

in my transparent coat
in my hat made of stones

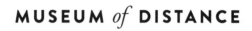

MUSEUM *of* **DISTANCE**

WINTER STORYBOARD

My mother loves only that which catches fire
and flame is the absence of plot. She irons her twenties

each bill crisp enough to slice the skin of those
who rummage her purse for mints. She spends

three days carving a white pygmy pumpkin—
It shall illuminate November, she says. And the month

after that? The pumpkin buckles and the long week
limps into the yard now salted with snow. Deer search

the earth for anything half-living. Memory calls
my mother's favorite integer brown, crafts a platter

from the limbs of a dead tree not dead to her.
Stray cats hug her humanly around the neck.

She hoards the rain and jars and foil and ferns, decades
of wrapping tissue too weak to wrinkle.

Can you hear the turtles building stones? She can.
Can you hear a leaf lying down on another leaf?

Each birdhouse in her garden falls from its post at least twice
every season, but she nails the lath with a surgeon's eye.

The birds forgive her. The birds return. My mother
mends her Christmas sweater and red thread traces her veins.

Like everyone, we mistake tragedy for comedy.
My mother altogether denies the arrival of January

and we prepare for her slumber. When she wakes
she will busy herself with the tasks of spring, and by then,

our grace, and sometimes our envy, will have grown back.

EPHEMERA

Even doubt is difficult, heated
　　slowly, cooked to softness, made
to sink in on itself, close around
　　its own emptiness, a pumpkin's only
trick. But isn't it somewhat obvious?
　　The candle wants to be a flower
lighting the porch, the flower wants to be
　　a small blue bird, and so on.
What you hear in your room
　　at night while you're wanting to be
your own plot of soft grass
　　is the world working around you—
it's quite a diligent machine!
　　You suspect it of telling many lies.
Yes, you are doubtful, sell
　　everything too cheaply, practically
give the world away, plastic cup by cup.
　　The chips of golden paint flaking off
that trophy are more embarrassing now.
　　Is it any wonder the world can't trust you?
Can you hear it breathing heavy
　　when you open the desk drawer of sleep
and you startle it by singing *wake up, wake up,*
　　this is how we tell a truth? Can you hear
it breathing now, climbing the stairs,
　　loosening its diamond-patterned tie,
the one you hate and try to hide,
　　the one that makes you dizzy?

NEWS HOUR AT LA VITA DOLCE

I know Eve grieved in the garden
when the clematis straightened itself out.
Many years after this, my neighbor scrapes
his house in the early morning and at noon apologizes
with sweat. He grieves the mailbox dented
by hail, the failing rhododendrons, the broken
windows, the passing youth of his daughter,
Lucy, four months old now.

Sweet communal patches of yellowing grass!
You are doing so much better these days!

I grieve for my brother who grieves for his ex-wife
who seems too young still to account for grief
which fills the room like a shovel falling. No one can
pad or prevent that clang, so I grieve for him, unaware
as I am of his intimate habits, the shadows passing over
his thin thumbs, his towel on the door with a faint odor.
The grand history of grief is defeated by my own history
of grief, which is defeated by me and my penchant for unusual
injury. Not to alarm you, but I am drowning in the real sense
in a sea of grief and if you're not listening carefully enough
you might think I'm saying *sea of greed*
and they could be the same thing.

As I child, I often slept in the middle of the day.
I remember it was obvious and easy. Now I worry
that I am indebted to every oak and elm on the planet,
and when can I possibly repay them all and with what?
Shhhhhhh, just listen to the sound of leaves,
hanging there and not falling. I am interested in this
fierce adhering and now I can see you
expected someone else entirely.
Are you disappointed?

You're right: all I am
is the sound of wind rearranging.

That my father has not yet died
but will someday and too soon.
How must I grieve for this?

Here is a Wednesday marked by rain.
Here is a raincoat, too large, hanging in the back
with empty shoulders and shiny buttons
like small faces.

YOU CAN FLY TOO CLOSE TO GOD

My mailman sees my letters,
who doesn't love me, how much.
The banker sees what I have
to lose. My doctor lays me down:
I breathe all the way in, all the way
out, past danger, past the shadow
where I'm unsure. You can fly too close
to God. People take off their shoes.
They fall asleep in the clouds.
The cable woman hugs the TV, kills
the sound. The man who unloads
oranges is unmoved by their perfection.
People turn my water off and on.
My teeth ache. Garbage men, gravediggers,
people in masks. Those who check a room
for poisonous fumes, manufacture
drains—there are secrets to defend!
One full day of rain: my shirt soaked through,
fingertips blue, *I don't trust the weatherman,*
I don't trust the weather. A passing stranger
slides an umbrella into my hand.
Warm and wet from use, the red umbrella
blooms—over me, under a thick white strip
of reliable sky, and over the ants
significant for their strength.

WHAT UNRAVELS: FOR ANGER

Everything a compromise, a half-
glass of milk that no one can
return to, a bone
the dog wants to bury
in distress, a dry elbow.

Someone could name
what we're going through.
No one could
ask it to be something else,
just for me, just for now.

Nothing could take
its place, not a fingernail
purpled from pain,
an undercooked casserole,
a bright orange sweater unraveling
on the crooked porch.

Not the threads
lying loose like soft fire,
the heat our own bodies make.
Not the light by the door—
always lit and phoning the flies.

I walk behind you in the wet field.
In the field, you walk in front.

I think of your body's subtle shift
north, what happened exactly.

TWO-STORY WITH A FINISHED BASEMENT

In the big house   on the long street
      there is a woman cleaning the stove
(with a toothbrush   with bleach)
      who has forgotten the man watching
television half-asleep one floor beneath her
      The man forgets the little boy
who plays with metal cars and soft dragons
      in his room two floors above
(in the light of a fisherman lamp)
      The little boy hears the channel change
from news to news   hears the bleach drop
      hears the close-up company of his cat
The little boy hears the faint drum
      of his own heart
and his mouth opens   (for that lonely song)

THE WIND CARRIED HIM AS IT CARRIED ME

When I open certain dreams they open me and leave
their melodies behind like buckshot: *careful, careful*
my grandmother sings while she stares down cancer and me, dancing
around the laundry pile mating all the black socks. It's impossible
not to feel betrayed by the little time left. Less and less.
Driving home I passed a boy on a bike on a bridge.
It was an old bridge, a young boy, a red bike. Autumn
was stretching out like he did that very morning in his own
soft bed. How can I explain? I stopped in evening
traffic and he moved beyond me and above the water and toward
a future he refused to share, but I never blamed him.
I loved the music of his leisurely pedaling. His unbrushed hair
was only his own but he didn't know how much this was true.
You already know how the wind carried him as it carried me
but whom do I salute now that I am sore and sighing? Does anyone
comfort anyone else as we pay on swelling debt? The children
I might have had are somersaulting across the backyards
of the city's ugliest houses and the river has exchanged its faithful tributary
for a new one. My friend the painter reminds me that everything
is a cycle: add a color to another color and another color comes.
I'm trying to savor every hue, like butter melting into yesterday's bread,
but what can I expect from myself or my allies full of grace
for the people who bag their groceries? *Don't crush the eggs.*
Don't crush the raspberries. In light of the many and simple laws
of physics, how can we call each other any closer?

THEIR HANDS STAINED A PALE GREEN

Someone threw a lemon into the lake
and it's been raining rind and pulp for days—
juicy, seedy, acidic and sour. No matter
how fast and long we drink, the ditches won't
dry up. Our open wounds are beginning
to sting. The grass is dying in bright yellow patches
and we face its affliction every time we leave
our houses, every time we return. Someone
once filled the fountain with pickles
and all the children's hands were stained
a pale green, but we kept calm,
used vinegar to our advantage, sweetened
a year's worth of bitterness on the tongue.
The city council sold cider by the truckload
to pay for all new drainage pipes. Garnish,
luxury, a knot of brightness on the ashen limb,
a lemon, one big lemon is falling from the sky
and we are stunned by clarity: the only way
to go is forward but we'd go back
if we could. We didn't know how hard
it would be to savor the simplest thing.

LILLIAN SAYS *DON'T READ THAT*

She is trying to save me
from *falsehood*, thinks the tabloids
are seeping in—that the way I stuff
a cookie into my innocent mouth is begging
for a photo, but photos are dangerous.

You think a baby can give birth
to another baby in a verdant suburban backyard.
That's how much the papers can fool you.

I think I'm moving my arms like this
and really they're moving
like this.

Someone is lying but no one remembers
who. Ink rubs off on everyone's hands.
Lillian said she saw the pope in the produce
aisle squeezing grapefruits, angry
because they all felt fake.

SCENE BEHIND A SHEET, WITH FLOWERS

Behold the wide body of a man.

He carries flowers: I can see the explosion

from his shoulder. *Are the flowers red?* I can't see

the man's nose; I draw one with a fleshy bridge,

two large nostrils like coins. Soft rim for a lip.

Suddenly a woman—I see the wisp of hair

important in a silhouette. He gives her the flowers

and her head bends to smell them.

How should I draw this? The woman repeats

my question. I spend days drawing her

feet: an arch fitting into a sandal, the shade

of an ankle-bone secret, the flowers unmistakably

red now. This is a holy business

knowing where to put each thing.

YOU NEVER KILLED A MAN

And you start all your Vietnam stories that way.
When we were young, we'd sit at your feet
to hear the one about the guys who cut in front
of you in the chow line—they'd been doing it
to everyone for weeks. A bunch of punks.
Get one behind, but don't get in front, you said.
And he punched you, right in your unfatherly face.
You threw him, beat him up.
Then his friends tried to kill you while you slept
in your bunk like a bachelor.
But not *really* you
because you are the man who put me on the school bus.
You are the man who helped me pronounce *Habukkuk.*
When your sister took us to Stonelick Lake
without any sunscreen and we returned wincing,
you spread aloe on our bare red backs,
on our over-freckled noses. On the tips of our ears,
you used your smallest finger.

UNQUIET IS MY OLD HOUSE

I have a steady hand and the knowledge
   of whose hands have first entered
these deep kitchen drawers and in what kind
   of pain. That's ridiculous, I know, to think
of Joe, who lived here over forty years,
   but holy is the art of making a sandwich
in the presence of his haunting, the black stain
   of his walking path rising up through weeks'
worth of scraping and four coats of finish.
   Visitors claim not to notice, but I insist
upon them seeing it and saying so. *It winds around*
   and through the doorways, plain as day! I am comforted
by the windows and their contribution, gaps enough
   for all the wind and whine. I layer up and think of
my mother's ghosts. When she was young she heard
   their steps at night, climbing the stairs of her
small house in California. Each tomato aging
   on my kitchen sill explains again its theory.
You can ripen and rot within the same few seconds.
   I hear my mother's voice and the unease of her
most vivid story since it's hardest to believe
   our own: the weight of a body at the end
of her bed that made her wake when she was six.
   She sat up, but no one was there. Just her
and her sisters—sleeping. *Since when,* I ask Joe,
   has their dreaming been as fearless?

MY HEART A BLUE BUTTON

I ate a pomegranate—it took six hours
then I rested. I swallowed the Nova Spy seeds

& a snow globe & four marbles I found.
My heart could be a glass apple by now!

No—smaller: a Dolcetto grape. I feel it ripen
in my chest while vessels nurse it

on their vines, I feel it wrinkle & relax.
Fits inside a button box now, easy to carry

& coddle, miss & misplace. My heart
a blue button that sleeps on my tongue,

my heart the tongue, small sea of new buds.
Faraway sister to the sieve combing the air

as I leap from trees that earn their rings
in utter stupefaction.

THE SLED

Imagine a boy with a tree inside him.

My grandfather told me the story only once and he looked down at his shoes. He was a child with a sled and an older friend from down the street could make him do anything. My grandfather grinds his teeth flat. My grandfather swallows nails. My grandfather climbs up and up a rickety ladder for sixty years and he always comes back down, though a man can sometimes lose his footing.

It is 1939. Boys believe someone just invented snow and every awful memory is so close to being a good one. His friend dares him down the hill and my grandfather hesitates, says no. His friend offers to go first and screams with glee on his way down, an echo for every *Are you chicken?* Because my grandfather lives, I know how close he is to death when he takes the dare and hits the tree, when the crash splits him in two at the groin, when the impact lodges a four-inch splinter in his rectum. My grandfather lives but not before he died a little. He cannot sit for months; he does not want to eat; his body stinks from infection. He can hardly stand himself and what he's done. *Imagine a boy with a tree inside him.*

As I write this, his tattoos are fading and his hair is thinning and I think about the sled, red and arresting like his blood in the snow, a darkened lake deepening around him, a fountain from the holy book of childhood half a chapter long.

A man can spend his whole life reading it.

A FOUNTAIN & THE MEASURED PASSES

The water holds more than it should
The air is thick with shadows that lean
Over the stone and into themselves
So I might find you
When I summon you to the fountain
On the darkest night of the year
On a still night a cold night
When I repeat the prayer of your body
When the birds vanish from the branches in mid-sleep
When I long to follow what leaves me

    You answer
    And I recognize the voice I've been hearing
    In faint and measured passes
    As my voice
    And it recognizes you

HOUSEWORK

Before this apartment smelling
of onions, before the boxes of carbon-
copied checks, the records that don't mean
anything for as long as I keep them
(and I keep them), before watching
my husband eat, one by one
each purple chip, the crumbs
on the sofa, our legs folded under
the coffee table; before all this
I loved you in your navy blue jacket
that never looked warm enough,
offering me a cheap cigar, holding a lighter
to my face as though you were feeding me
oranges, which you could have done
(I would have accepted). For the third night
in a row I wake to a memory of myself
before my life as it has turned out
to be, a good life, one I believe
I chose, and still I miss you
but so what? This frame, this fire red
serving dish, this parade of books, everything
gets dusty, then I wipe it down like a decade
I can't believe has passed, then everything
gets dusty again. Remember the night
we walked that cluttered college town street
until it got light again? We smoked cigars
and ignored the cold. We felt young but already
the regret. We believed in our own
instincts: walk closer, slowly. The only thing
I knew for sure was that I wouldn't ever
love you less, despite the distance or decision
I knew would divide us. Sure enough
the branches above us weakened and the moon

began to slim down and the road narrowed
to a single lane, then a driveway, then a door.
Even then I silently insisted as I do now.

WENDING FISH & THE MUSSELS

Sorrow can be heavier
than any celebration of tenderness.

Sometimes it's the opposite
and there is a man at the pier

with no fish at the end
of his line, no bait either.

Come to me he says about nothing
to no one though the fish listen.

I look, with him, out there.
I am trying to see one league

past where he is barely able.
I am trying to carry what is left

of his last days back
to the banks no longer

populated by mussels. The heart,
it turns out, can break in half

from happiness
as easily as it does from pain.

Sometimes, then, this man
is my father. He is someone's.

The wending fish are mine, please,
the mussels yours, and now I see

how this man prefers the infinite
sound of a singular wave.

SOMETHING WENT BANG INSIDE ME

I've never even been to the ocean.
How does it sound in the dark?
I wish you were here
to see this: I wear coats with fringe.
Something just went bang inside me
and all my doubt leaks right out.
I smell the neighbor's exhaustion.
Once I out-swam a wave.
I held my breath for six hours.
This is possible. Everything is.
Do you know who you're talking to?
I didn't steal a thing—not money
or sunscreen or the girl
with almond eyes. Nothing
was actually stolen. Do people see me
as a big clown in a small swim suit?
Am I accidentally near the beginning?
The sunset followed me to the sand.
This is my beach. I only took
what was mine though I admit
my sense of ownership is skewed.

FINAL CURTAIN
FOR THE CORNFIELD

You are a broad poem

an umber-colored poem

a poem that could wave its arms
and take me in.

You are brittle
from needing rain
so I come with water
down the dusty lanes
in Waynesville
to unfold you.

I ride my bike
along your ribbon of road
and say so little
I disappear.

The stars live close.

The world is bright with indifference.

In the future, no one sees
anything move the breeze.

Sliver of a poem

poem-of-the-earth

I've spread you out
too thin, I know.
I hear the birds
on your behalf.

I'll gather you again.

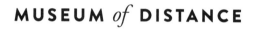

MUSEUM *of* DISTANCE

TO HEAR THE BLACKBIRDS LIVE, TO SEE THE END

I am here and there is nothing
to say. What we require
is silence; what silence requires
is that I go on. I have nothing
to say and I am saying it.
We need not fear these silences.
A New Yorker knows he needs
the Kansas in him, nothing
but wheat. Our poetry now
is the realization that we possess
nothing and thus need not
fear its loss. The past
might reappear and appear
to be the present. It is free
and so are we. Poetry, a piece
of music, is proof that our delight
lies in not possessing anything.
Each moment happens. Unlike the snail
we carry our homes within us, to stay
beautiful. Nothing
more than nothing can be said.
Blackbirds rise from a field, alive
and significant. To hear
the blackbirds live, to see the end,
to understand you, to ask and think
and feel the end. To say more.
Clearly we are beginning to get nowhere.
If one is making, the one making
must love and be patient—be made.
We make our lives by what
we love and this explains how
after several years of working alone
I began to feel lonely. This made me

the most. I decided only quiet
sounds to be truth, but quiet sounds
were loneliness. I still feel this way.
I begin to hear new sounds—they are
as audible as thinking them, they
are new, nowhere, a story.
If there are no questions, there are
no answers. You'll see, I've seen nothing.
Here we are now: somewhere else,
more and more, nowhere.
We were nowhere, we are slowly nowhere.
Here we are now: somewhere else,
a beginning, the feeling of beginning.
If anybody is sleepy, let him go to sleep.
If anybody, let him go. If anybody
is sleepy, let him go to sleep.

PALM HEARTS

In order to properly cook asparagus, you must first choose it from a waist-high field of leafage and greenery, some with very tempting names, such as kale and ladyfingers and shallot, and your lover's favorite: palm hearts. It is crucial that you first *choose* asparagus, much as you would choose love, and then that you choose the specific stalks that suit you and your tastes, much as you would choose a specific lover from another field of candidates, each one unaware of your scrupulous eye but also unexplainably nervous. *Where is the bow tie I saved for such a day?* It is also true, however, that the asparagus is choosing you and so you are really only doing fifty percent of the choosing. There are reasons to choose a slender stalk and many people do; there are reasons to choose a thicker stalk and many people do. It is possible to choose poorly early on, after you've already chosen the shoes you will wear to temporarily leave your lover, requester of palm hearts, after you've chosen the store, and the route you will take there, and after you've chosen your cart from yet another field of carts (empty and open and waiting to be chosen)—it is possible to choose what you might realize later is the wrong asparagus and still enjoy it since really the choosing has less to do with choosing correctly, as you'll learn and relearn every time you eat, and more to do with the expectation you're secretly choosing, and even more secretly, only half-choosing. Your lover has requested palm hearts, which is the loveliest vegetable you've ever imagined: a heart offering its palm, a palm beating its heart, a palm *using* another palm to cover its heart, the heart showing through.

TOO MUCH AT DUSK

Your lungs are like a whale's
but you want better. Someone asked
how you are doing & sweetie you are fine.
A little tired. I like your hat, the color of papaya.
I like that it's too large. When you brought down
that box from the attic, I knew in my heart-shaped head
it was filled with more boxes. I reserved
the smallest one for the last day we spend together
when you & I are both alive in the sun, which they tell me
will weaken like a battery. I love you least
in the morning but only because I love you too much
at dusk, so when we last speak, mid-day after a lunch
of fruit & cucumbers, I hope there's a plane
flying too low in the sky & the grass is too green
to bear, the bells far too loud.

TONIGHT I'LL SHAVE YOUR FACE

Not because I do it well or quickly
  but because it slows us both
to notice how the skin is delicate,
  determined. You'll look forward
at the wall, feel the razor touch down
  where I sweep it steadily across that jaw line
clenched in sweet suspense. You'll trust me
  to do this because in the morning
I'll boil your breakfast eggs. You'll trust me
  because I've heard you talk in your sleep—
something about your father's camera
  dropped in the muddy creek. Lately
your stubble comes from self-defeat
  and I know where *that* comes from too
and so you'll trust me with this razor,
  with the blade that cuts the rough
dark hair and leaves instead a shadow.

THE BETTER TO SEE YOU MY DEAR

The grey & drizzle, droplets on a tree
in early spring, clear & frozen eyes,

absence of what is bright & warm,
how we know we are only our own.

Around the south end of the house
the loosened gutter again, the sidewalk

beneath it a deadly sheet of ice. Amble
slowly & be ready to catch yourself.

It never rains, it always rains, we need
more rain, we've had too much.

The neighbor's dog ate down another bush
along the fence. *The better to see you my dear.*

Cars speed by past parents pulling
children in wagons of every color,

past parents holding those small hands,
skin thin with innocence. The stop signs

shine red & illuminate what might be true.
That every plate in the kitchen is a little dirty,

every cup ringed with another day's coffee,
the towels a bit too rough, the bar of neon soap

with hair on it. Everything in the freezer
is melted, everything in the refrigerator is frozen,

I'm not kidding. Lettuce wilting hour by hour
in a see-through crisper. Who is at the door,

when are we leaving, why are we late, where
are we going by ourselves but together via

different modes of transportation? Imagine:
a person finding & repairing every crack

in all the sidewalks of this vast city, sidewalks
that groan, shrink & expand again

with the weather & weight of all the people.
What would be an appropriate salary for such

an endless task & who would be her apprentice?
A dog so thin & hungry for attention you could

feel each rib & stare. That same dog years later:
thick-haired, large-chested, well-fed, loved absolutely.

The labor pains of a woman who has endured
them before. A father riven with despair for his son

riven with pain. Cups of tea with & without a fog
of milk. Leaves of a young thriving fern that soak up

the window's light from the hours of eleven
until six, when ever so gently the sun

covers its burning face. Open up a map,
any map, flat or relief & point to any place—there

you'll sense it before you ever see it:
the quietude, the expectation of extremes

that permits a baby, months old, to erupt
with joy when she distinguishes for the first time

her own nose from all the noses of the people
who have held her in front of the mirror,

this same mirror, her neck a little stronger every day;
& the sadness that the ground accepts

when the smallest of all birds mistakes a window
for another possible world in which to fly,

one wing above the current,
one wing below.

CONFESSION NEAR THE HOLLYHOCK

Your voice is not blue.
  It doesn't taste like a blackberry
to me. It doesn't move
  like a cloud over a calm sea
or hover lightly at the cliff.
  It doesn't hover brightly
bent toward the door.
  When the window promises
a future, I assume
  I'm welcome there:
posture imperfect, reeds
  for wrists, all the dross.

  Your voice is not blue,
not light blue or dark.
  There's no spark
when you speak, no needle
  of delight. I say your name
in silence and lick the letters
  back. Your voice belongs
at the mouth of an empty cup,
  but I drink it down.
I call everything forward,
  give my faint body to the grasses.
Any luck I might possess.
  All my awkwardness. I see
something move near
  the hollyhock—

I lose everything
  with both hands.
The sky looks less
  and less like a door
anyone could push open
  or pass through.

NEW HISTORIES: WHAT TO DO WITH MY ARMS

We look out our large front window
and see the same bright-chested cardinal
hopping on a thick branch felled from high winds.
You dream about a tornado, our house swirling in eights.
I find seeds in our food for the next ten years.
One day I wake up and the waking feels familiar
but I've never seen *you* before, or these white dishes.
You're gone all day
and I can't remember what you look like
despite the threads of coarse dark hair
on the couch and in the carpet. I collect them
and blow specific wishes from my fingertips.
The first wish is for you to sing to me.
The last wish is for you to sing to me.
You come home, you come home
but I don't know what to do with my arms.
I wear the wrong socks, the really long ones you can't find the ends of.
I like your singing and stumble into love with you, ask you
to marry me right here under the kitchen stars.
You mention how we're already married but say we weren't—
say we just met, barely know middle names, are nervous
to laugh too hard at our new joke. Say we're shy
with what is ours and most tender. See, it's already morning.
Let me surprise you with what I remember.
Another morning. What I'm willing to forget.

PARALLAX & THE PRESERVATION OF SPACE & TIME, OR HOW YOU MISTOOK THAT LEAF FOR LINT

I watched my grandma, single-breasted,
  linger in our ranch house—a living phantom
not unlike the kind that fleck your vision.
  What can be seen with two eyes,
with one? I watched her fade
  but not before I watched my father
clean & dress the open wound gaping
  in her chest as if she'd been to war & back.
She died, I remember my surprise
  at how cold her body felt: a soft machine
quickly closing down. Never did I think that
  that same sickness, a polished scythe,
could be so choosy—to think it went
  for your brown eyes. It's never clear,
but the world is even fuzzier since your
  diagnosis: everyone is droopy, half-erased.
It's hard to find & shake the hands of lifelong
  friends. Even though I'm tempted to say
size does not much matter, I know you'd
  disagree. I can hear you asking now: how
to preserve our vision when our vision
undermines? How to not be terrified
  when pouring wine?

BELUGA PATRIOT

Teenagers in the corner complex set off their stash
of firecrackers in one hot spell and now, so near
to midnight, the sidewalk is ablaze with their cursing
and mine, their drunken *Happy Birthday Americas,*
my grey rainbow of sobriety. I stop my bike
at our street's end to wait it out. I try to trust the average
citizen with explosives, but all I can conjure are stories
of horror and the stumps of once lively thumbs.
Sometimes the nearest thing I can reach
is reproach and guilt for this is even further down.
I've said hello to these boys before, perched
on their second-story balcony, cups of butts
surrounding their chairs like luminaries.
When I wave I am often walking our dog.
I am always rushed. My love, you hardly look me
in the face these days and not with any focus so I blush
when others do. Despite my fear of most things
dangerous, I am more and more persuaded
by tonight's display of verve: I like the ones that *begin*
with detonation then hang their dust-like willow shoots
in the darkest part of the sky as if to perfect
the fade. I'm willing to share *this* danger
with *these* boys. I'm willing to wave as if
to a president, to wish on—one by one—
every star they set on fire.

AREA CODES: A POEM WITH PIE

Later, another day, the cockleburs
will hang on to our dresses. But for now
we share Ohio and live as if we always will—
firefly cities inside one net. I watch you build
a banana cream pie in Cleveland and sob.
You make the whipping cream three times
unsure of how you keep getting it wrong.
Slowly you slice the bananas on a paper plate
until you see the one with a blackened core,
eaten through by a bug. What doesn't get
ruined? Layer by layer, you build a pie
for your boyfriend's birthday, crying and baking,
as if the one required the other. When the shiny
new mixer doesn't work, you use the old one,
kept below. The new mixer is as red as your feet
when you've worn those soft moccasins too long
but the old mixer is the one you trust. You unstrangle it.
I can feel the late-summer lake breeze blowing in.
The kitchen curtain billows between this
and whatever is next, and I'm thinking
you should double the recipe.

WE'RE NOT HUNGRY & WE'RE NEVER HUNGRY

Your face in the baking aisle stares
    at me from behind all those boxes.
        My heart, an egg white.
    Your body, brighter than flour.
Don't be confused: I'm not making a cake
    out of you, or asking you to give more
        than you promised. I measure closely.
    I imagine us at the kitchen counter
our apron strings looped together loosely
    our fingers rough with salt.
        We spend the whole day baking
    until there's nothing left to mix in.
Our feet ache from standing. We wash our hands
    until they break open. The windows
        are splattered with milk.
    All of this is familiar, like we've made this
life before. We remember how we loved it.
    We're not hungry and we're never hungry.
        No, wait—we're starving. Yes,
    we eat and eat, the pastries and pies!
We fill ourselves up with parfaits!
    In the morning, we taste regret.
        The kitchen's still a mess, we can't find
clean knives. Now, we only want a simple breakfast,
    to live happily through an ordinary day
        and we swear we'll be thankful
    for every bit of sweetness we're offered.
We are humbled by the empty plate,
    strengthened by fasting, but we leave
        the oven on—

ONE THOUSAND WORDS FOR MY FATHER

Before we left for the west
you surprised me with a Nikon
that's heavy in my hand.
Unfocused, I shoot: you posed
at the pier; the seals sleeping on the rock pile,
slippery and babbling; a young Spanish couple
groping on the boat tour around Alcatraz;
by accident, my left leg. In Monterey
I learn from a white wooden sign
that police can fine me for a butterfly kill,
five-hundred dollars, no matter if it smacks
the window or I chase it down.
Don't waste film, you say.
Get that California mountain.
Get the sunset behind it.
I take a picture—
not of the sunset or the mountain,
or the live butterflies, papery and bright,
that rest on the balcony banisters—
but of the wooden sign, newly repainted.
      I take the picture while driving away.
      The sign and the city narrow behind us.
      Overhead, gulls escort our car
      to the city limit, and one small boy waves
      from his yard: hoping I live far from here,
      that I'll frame this, him with his dog.

WITH THE DESERT MICE IN MIND

Every answer is the darkness. So our hands are hard
to explain. Stars brighten our silence & the desert
expands to absorb each echo in our bones. A mouse

scuttles crevices of slickrock under Orion's Belt.
The mice are making plans, simple ones but goodly.
They agree with us: anything that must be *said*

is treason. We hide our headlamps when the jeep
blares by, a search team for that teenage boy.
Questions move across the sky—comets

we could name, we might name them.
Every answer is the darkness so I stand too long
near the edge of the mesa cliff & mangled veins

of thirsty shrubs considering flight. The plans of mice
(an eyelash wide) & those tiny hearts are beacons
calling me back. They call me back.

SPACING EFFECT

Your shadow stretches for the stonemason's yard.

The room closes in one twitch at a time,
slip-and-stall of conversation. Let me explain

how I dream of deep snow

clear a path for deliveries
and wait. In the dairy aisle I count cartoon cows.

I know by her exhaustion when my mother
has been to the coast and back.

She touches the water with her gloves on.

I lotion up on the hour
and divide the teas and contemplate peregrination.

In this way I am organized
keeping the wind in my bluest things.

I sleep near a shark's tooth.

I am hungry and live on the quarter notes
soaring up and up from the aviaries

of Euclid's abandoned buildings. I cough
the evening smog and pray near the eastern window

as it shudders for the train and its roar.
Dangerous is the morning's work and difficult.

AERIAL VIEW

School of sorrow, skill of joy
What I arrange & avoid, what I disregard
What I stare down   no   what I disbelieve
The brightest stars & their best angles
        I record my findings
        But I give them back   or I plan to

Your mother stands on that broken toe again
Rising the bread in silence   a prayer
Near the gossamer curtains my own mother darns
        Two days it takes her
        Nose to the needle

Considering the clouds themselves
What they can manage
I follow the trail, I follow you
To see the lights   but I never do see
        Each detail misleading

With or without the relentless heat
Your grandfather's groves   those neon oranges

The river in which my sister carries me
On her shoulders
        Above the mackerel & above the blue

THE ENGINE OF ONE DEEP BREATH

There is a fire on the lake—
out there, far out
past the point where you could swim with the engine
of one deep breath, way past that.
A fire of ideas burning
into metaphor, rain turning back
on white-capped hats to salute
what the sun can't shine through.

That the water carries itself and us
newly saved.

Like children, the orange cackle
of flames is carried farther into the darkness
into corners, cornered now.
They are small plastic boats.
No, not boats: buoys.
Not buoys. Nothing
wants to float forever, not really.

ACKNOWLEDGMENTS

Thank you to the editors of the journals in which these poems first appeared, sometimes in different versions and with different titles.

Anti-: "The Science of Longevity" and "Corrosion Theory"
Brevity: "The Sled"
The Burnside Review: "Diagram Including Time & Bananas" and "Area Codes: A Poem with Pie"
Cimarron Review: "We're Not Hungry & We're Never Hungry"
The Cincinnati Review: "Winter Storyboard," winner of the Robert and Adele Schiff Poetry Prize, selected by Don Bogen
The Citron Review: "Palm Hearts"
Colorado Review: "Astonishment for the Sparrows," "Hound," "Proof" and "You Can Fly Too Close to God"
Connotation Press: "Breathing Down the House" and "Unquiet Is My Old House"
Cutbank: "Aerial View" in Issue 70 and in *Cutbank's 40th Anniversary Anthology*
Dogwood: "Allergies" and "You Never Killed a Man"
Hunger Mountain: "Between Land & Water," winner of the Ruth Stone Poetry Prize, selected by Matthew Dickman
Iron Horse Literary Review: "Lillian Says *Don't Read That*"
Parcel: "Something Went Bang Inside Me"
Quarterly West: "The Wind Carried Him As It Carried Me" and "A Cup of Salt Consumes the Sea"
Slice: "Ephemera"
The Southeast Review: "Beluga Patriot"
The Sow's Ear Poetry Review: "Tonight I'll Shave Your Face"
The St. Petersburg Review: "Shortcoming"
The Tusculum Review: "The Better To See You My Dear"
Western Humanities Review: "Hymn for the Leaping Pig" and "Origin & the Apple Bruised," winners of the Utah Writers' Contest, selected by Peter Cole
Zone 3: "Each Leg a Good Root," "Persistence of Vision," and "Tragedies Near Weeping Rock"

The following poems appear online, sometimes in different forms, as part of a collaborative art project, called SPARK: Art from Writing, Writing from Art.

"News Hour at La Vita Dolce"
"The Storm, My Chest So Close to the Spade"
"Spacing Effect"

"To Hear the Blackbirds Live, To See the End" is an erasure poem written from John Cage's 1959 "Lecture on Nothing."

I am incredibly lucky to have worked with a host of wonderful teachers and mentors over the years. Many thanks to James Reiss, Mark Halliday, Jill Allyn Rosser, Sharmila Voorakkara, Mary Ruefle, Ralph Angel, Jody Gladding, and Leslie Ullman. Special thanks to Natasha Sajé, whose support and guidance have made all the difference.

Many friends have cheered me on and inspired me to create. In most cases, the wind has scattered us to different places, but I'm thankful for the time we spent (and still spend) talking about life and writing, often over a cup of tea. Thanks to Adam Tavel, Laura Portalupi, Kristen Lillvis, Stacy K.H. Perrou, Sarah Engler Pirtle, Emily Zaborniak, Carrie Oeding, Angie Mazakis, Katie Sheehan, Malcolm Campbell, Jon Cone, Shawn Fawson, Erica Stewart Martin, Jessi Lydon, Lance Newman, Joanna Pham, and Christine Seifert.

I am thrilled that the stunning art of Honora Jacob covers this book. Thank you kindly for this partnership, Honora.

I'm indebted to the editors at Zone 3 Press for their support, and I'm grateful to Angela Ball for selecting this collection as the winner of the Zone 3 Press First Book Award.

Thanks to the people at Gathering Place in Athens, Ohio. I truly value the years (2003-2008) we spent together at that table sharing poems; that time and those poems left an indelible impression on me. Special thanks to Barbara Roush and Michael McDowell.

My deepest gratitude goes to my parents, Tom and Kay, for the longevity and constancy of their love and support (in all things, including writing). They are grounded, kind, generous, hardworking, and funny; I'm doing well if I possess a tenth of any of that. And thanks to Emily and Aaron, my older siblings, who have always taken good care of me, even paved a path for me, in this precarious world. I learn from all of you and love you dearly.

All my love and thanks to Eric Kramer, a great partner on the trail and a great mind.